GOD MADE ME
FOR
WORSHIP

Helping Children Understand Church

Jared Kennedy

Illustrated by
Trish Mahoney

"Be filled with the Spirit, speaking to one another with psalms, hymns, and songs from the Spirit. Sing and make music from your heart to the Lord, always giving thanks to God the Father for everything, in the name of our Lord Jesus Christ."

Ephesians 5:18–20

Dear Parent or Caregiver,

I wrote this book to give you a way to introduce your children to public worship. When you think of explaining a worship service, you might say something like this: "First, we sing. Then, we listen to the sermon." But most worship gatherings involve more than music and preaching. When the church gathers, we follow a rhythm—or liturgy—of *call* and *response*. It's like a big game of follow the leader. We hear God speak and then we move in response to him.

Maybe you've noticed this rhythmic back and forth in your own church's gatherings. First, you hear God's Word call to you—perhaps in what we describe literally as the "call to worship"—but then also in words of blessing or assurance and finally in the sermon's words of instruction. Then, after you hear from God's Word, you respond by lifting your voice in song, greeting others, giving, or by shouting, "Amen!"

We repeat this back and forth every week when we come to church, just as Christians have for hundreds of years. During the Reformation, John Calvin saw a need to help the church rehearse gospel rhythms when it gathered for worship.[1] His liturgy followed three movements:

- *Adoration*—Drawn from Isaiah 6, this rhythm reveals God as holy and calls upon sinners to respond with a cry for mercy.
- *Renewal*—Rooted in the burning bush story of Exodus 3, this rhythm begins with reading and teaching God's Word then calls for a response of reverence and humility.
- *Commitment*—This rhythm, based in Luke 24, involves seeing Christ's glory and participating in it as we gather around the table for communion.

God Made Me for Worship walks kids through each of these rhythms. My goal is that they'll see and learn how *all the parts of worship work together to tell the gospel story*. The words we use to describe the parts of worship and the particular orders of worship we follow differ from church to church. But a wide variety of traditions view gathered worship as a weekly rehearsal of the good news. And that's my prayer, that the children who read this book will learn to love and enjoy their church's regular gatherings, because in worship they hear Christ speak and then by faith respond.

With joy in Christ,
Jared Kennedy

[1] To learn more about this history, see Timothy J. Keller, "Reformed Worship in the Global City," in *Worship by the Book*, ed. D. A. Carson (Grand Rapids, MI: Zondervan, 2002), 193-239, and Mike Cosper, *Rhythms of Grace: How the Church's Worship Tells the Story of the Gospel* (Wheaton, IL: Crossway Books, 2013), 117-50.

Mrs. Jackson walked the fourth graders to the front of the sanctuary after their class. Pastor Barnabas was waiting there for them.

"You can ask your question now, Alice," said Mrs. Jackson.

Alice stepped forward, and her face lit up.

"I love going to church!" she said,
"but sometimes it's confusing."

Alice's classmates nodded.

"First, we stand. Then, we sit.
One minute we're singing loudly.
The next minute, we have to be still and quiet.
Shhhhhh! No talking.
Then, all at once, everyone stands,
shakes hands, and talks to other people again.

Here's my question.
**Why are there so many
different parts to a church service?"**

"And why does it have to be so long?" asked Henry.
Mrs. Jackson looked embarrassed,
but Pastor Barnabas just smiled and laughed.

"That's a great question, Alice," said Pastor Barnabas. Then he sat down with Mrs. Jackson's class in a row of chairs next to the big stained-glass window.

You can read about what Isaiah saw in Isaiah 6.

"All the parts of worship tell the gospel story.

It might seem long, but when you understand it, it's the best story ever told. Let me tell you about it:

In the Bible, there's a story about a prophet named Isaiah who lived a long time before Jesus was born. A prophet is someone who heard God's words and told them to the people.

Isaiah was sad because a good king, King Uzziah, had died. So Isaiah went up to the temple to pray and worship God. When Isaiah was in the temple, something amazing happened. He saw the Lord!"

"When we come to church each week, it's sometimes hard to pay attention. We can be worried about our schoolwork, what our friends are doing, or even about how long the service will be." Pastor Barnabas winked at Henry as he said the last part.

"But just as God called Isaiah away from his sadness to see God at the temple, we begin our church services with a

call to worship.

The worship leader reminds us to **STOP,** pay attention, and listen to God."

"When Isaiah saw God in the temple, what else do you think he saw?" asked Pastor Barnabas.

"Did he see some angels?" asked Jalen.

"Yes," said Pastor Barnabas.

Praise and Adoration

"But they looked different from the baby angels you might see on Christmas cards. Each had six wings. With two wings, the angels covered their faces. With two, they covered their feet. And with two, they flew. The angels shouted words of **praise and adoration**: "The Lord our God is the Most Holy One. He is beautiful and completely separate from sin.""

"God is the best!"
said Pastor Barnabas.
"He deserves our praise.
When we go to church, we sing like the angels:
'How great is our God! Praise ye the Lord,
the Almighty, the King of creation!'"

Worship begins
with God.
What did you
sing about God
in church
this week?

As the angels shouted praises, their voices shook the temple's doors and floors. The building filled up with dust and smoke. Isaiah was terrified! "I'm doomed," he cried, "I say that I love God with my lips, but then I don't obey him."

"When we see how holy our God is, we can also see our sin and disobedience," explained Pastor Barnabas. "When we go to church, we say prayers of **confession and lament**. We tell God we're sorry for sin and sad about our broken world."

I'm Sorry

Is there a sin you need to confess today?

Alice gasped and covered her eyes.
She was frightened for Isaiah.

"What happened to him?" she asked. "What did God do?"

"God didn't punish Isaiah," said Pastor Barnabas.

"When Isaiah confessed his sins, God sent one of his angels to the
temple. The angel flew down to the altar. You see, God had shown
his people just what kind of sacrifices to bring in order to say,
'Thank you, God!' or 'I love you, God!' or 'I'm sorry, God!'
The people burned their gifts and sacrifices for God upon the altar.

So, God sent his angel down to the altar to take a coal from the fire.
The angel touched it to Isaiah's lips, and he said,

'Your sins are forgiven.'"

"When we trust in Jesus," said Pastor Barnabas, "God heals our broken relationship with him. The Holy Spirit helps us to love God and to treat our friends, family, and neighbors with love and kindness too.

We remember how Jesus fills us with his love and kindness when we **welcome** one another and say hello. In some churches they call this time, '**passing the peace**.'

We shake hands, give hugs, and say, 'Peace be with you.'"

Welcome

Henry laughed from the back of the class. "I know this part," he said.

Then, he came to the front, shook Pastor Barnabas's hand, and spoke in his most grown-up voice:

How are you?

"I'm fine," laughed Pastor Barnabas.

Who did you talk to during the welcome time at church this week?

Ministry of the Word

Next Pastor Barnabas said,
"You see, we come to church to hear
the gospel, the story of God's good news."

God is good and great.
We are sinners.
Jesus saves us from sin.

"We hear the good news read,
and we hear it preached.

When a worship leader reads the Bible out loud,
he might say, 'This is God's Word.'
And we'd respond by saying, 'Thanks be to God!'

Then, when I'm preaching the good news,
the people shout, 'That's right! Amen!'"

Communion

"Christians also remember the gospel by taking communion. The servers say: **'This is Christ's body. This is his blood.'** Christians eat and drink to remember how Jesus died for our sins."

You can read about communion in Luke 22:19-20.

"I think I understand," said Alice.

"God made us to worship him. And all the parts of our worship work together to tell the story of the gospel."

"That's right," said Pastor Barnabas.

"But Jesus didn't just die for our sins. On the very next Sunday, God raised him from the dead.

Obedience

Jesus is alive!

And because Jesus lives, we can live
in obedience to him. We do that
by **confessing our faith** and
serving one another.

One way we serve one another is by
sharing our money with the church.
We give money to the church. The church
helps others know Jesus better."

**Many churches
confess their
common faith by
saying the Lord's
Prayer or the
Apostles' Creed
when they gather.**

TITHES

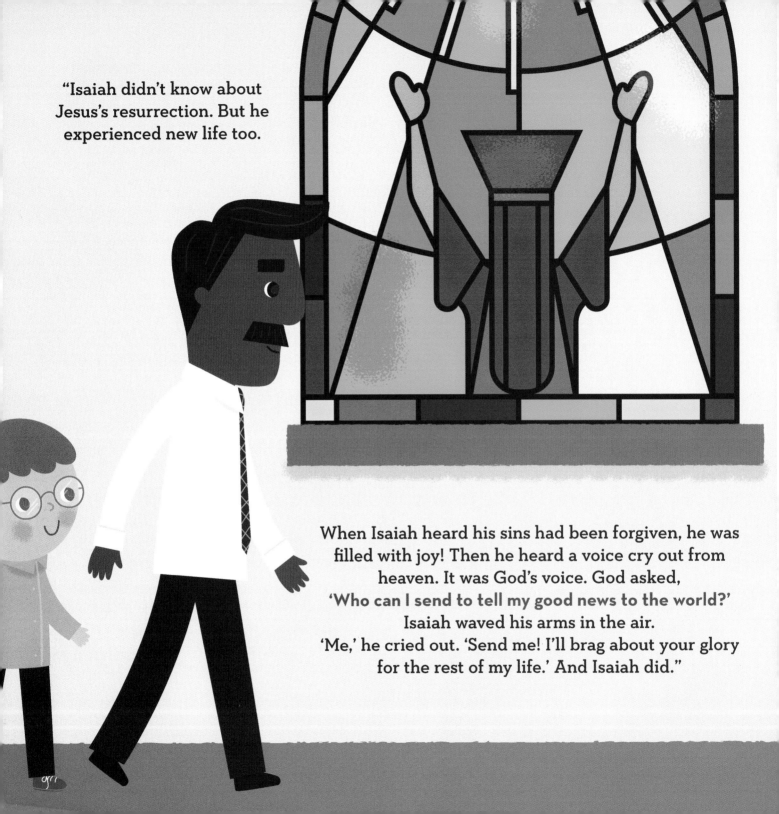

"Isaiah didn't know about Jesus's resurrection. But he experienced new life too.

When Isaiah heard his sins had been forgiven, he was filled with joy! Then he heard a voice cry out from heaven. It was God's voice. God asked, 'Who can I send to tell my good news to the world?' Isaiah waved his arms in the air. 'Me,' he cried out. 'Send me! I'll brag about your glory for the rest of my life.' And Isaiah did."

Pastor Barnabas walked with the class toward the doors at the back of the church. Alice's mom was waiting for her there.

"Worship doesn't stop because you're going home," he said.

"Just like Isaiah, God sends us out to tell the good news to others."

Benediction

Alice bounded down the front steps ahead of her mother.

She couldn't wait to tell her dad how all the parts of church worship tell the story of the gospel.

As she hopped into the back seat,
Pastor Barnabas heard her ask,

"Dad, have you heard about Isaiah?"

Teaching Kids to
WORSHIP
EVERY DAY

This book is designed to teach your children how every part of a church worship service tells the story of the gospel. But God hasn't just commanded us to worship him when we come to church. The Bible teaches us to praise the Lord during every part of our day. God wants us to teach our kids to live fully worshipful lives.

In Psalm 78:4, the songwriter, Asaph, declares: "We will . . . tell the coming generation the glorious deeds of the Lord, and his might, and the wonders that he has done."

Asaph is an example both of a parent who led his children in worship and of a leader who led the community in worship. Another songwriter, David, describes a similar scene in Psalm 145:

> One generation commends your works to another;
> they tell of your mighty acts.
> They speak of the glorious splendor of your majesty—
> and I will meditate on your wonderful works.
> They tell of the power of your awesome works—
> and I will proclaim your great deeds.
> They celebrate your abundant goodness
> and joyfully sing of your righteousness. (Psalm 145:4-7 NRSV)

This is God's desire for us. One generation *declares* God's wonder and works to the next. How do you do that as a mom, dad, grandparent, or caregiver? Here are just a few encouragements.

1 Slow down and say thanks for what God has given you.

David says, "I will meditate on your wonderful works" (Psalm 145:5). One of God's wonderful works is your children. The young boy or girl in your care is fearfully and wonderfully made (Psalm 139:14). So the next time he or she makes you laugh or says something cute and you're tempted to pull out your phone and share that moment with the world . . . instead, just take it in. Enjoy it. And remember the Creator who gave you this gift. Stop and say thanks.

2 Put off complaining and put on a life of praise.

Kids will wear you out! When they're babies, it's those midnight feedings and constant diaper changes. As they grow, you're running here and there to practice or clubs. Helping a child grow up is hard. And do you know what we're tempted to do? We're tempted to complain about the gifts God has given us. We're complaining *about* them when—according to these passages—we should be telling, proclaiming, celebrating, and joyfully singing about God's goodness and love *to* them. So when you're tempted to complain, stop and remember that God loves you. Then celebrate him before your kids. Put some good music on and sing about God as you drive in the car. Read a Bible storybook before bedtime and pray a little prayer of thanks as you tuck your child in at night. Put off complaining, redirect your heart, and enjoy yourself as you're celebrating God! Expressive joy in Christ makes his message believable for our children. You are the curriculum your child will learn most fully. So put on a life of praise. It truly is a good thing to praise the Lord (Psalm 92:1).

3 Finally, encourage your kids to be responsive and expressive!

You shouldn't demand outward expression from your kids in worship, but you can encourage it. The Scriptures call everyone to clap their hands to the Lord. It's a universal appeal (Psalm 47:1). So we should be clear with our children that God is calling them to respond to him as well. Invite your kids to respond to God with their bodies by raising their hands in worship or bending their knees in prayer. Use this book or other tools to explain why we worship the way we do (Exodus 13:8). You have the privilege and responsibility to show your kids the greatness, power, and glory of Jesus. So take time to talk about the words we sing on Sunday. Take time to ask questions about what a song means and how its words apply to your child's life. By asking, you can discover how much your kids understand.

Try it this week:

1. Explain a common worship practice to your children. You could pick one that is described in this book or pick another that is common in your church community.

Here are brief explanations for two common worship practices that were not described in detail as part of the order of worship I wrote about here.

Lifting Hands. We sometimes raise our hands when we sing or pray. Read 1 Timothy 2:8, and then explain how it is good to lift your hands in worship. We don't lift our hands to become holy. Rather, we lift our hands as an expression of what God is doing in us. Lifting our hands shows that God is holy (different from us), and he has made us holy (different from the world).

Giving. Each Sunday, churches include giving as a part of their worship service by passing an offering plate or basket. Read 2 Corinthians 9:6-14. Explain to your children that all we have comes from God and belongs to God, so we can joyfully give back to God and his church through our offerings.

2. Read Psalm 98 together as a family. Then answer these questions: Who and what is worshiping God in this song? How are they worshiping God? What parts of their bodies do they use? What instruments do they use? Why do they worship God in this way?

This book is dedicated to

Dr. Robert K. Wetmore

Forman Christian College, Punjab, Pakistan

and

Mike Cosper

The Narrativo Group, Louisville, KY

These two men, in their different ways, are committed to cultivating godly affections in the next generation. Thank you both for teaching me about Christian worship.

New Growth Press, Greensboro, NC 27404
Text Copyright © 2020 by Jared Kennedy
Illustration Copyright © 2020 by Trish Mahoney

Unless otherwise noted, all Scripture quotations were taken from The Holy Bible, New International Version® NIV® Copyright © 1973, 1978, 1984, 2011 by Biblica, Inc.™

Art and Design: Trish & Patrick Mahoney

ISBN: 978-1-64507-048-1

Library of Congress Cataloging-in-Publication Data on file

Printed in India

27 26 25 24 23 22 21 20   1 2 3 4 5